THE PELICANS

BY
WILLIAM R. SANFORD
CARL R. GREEN

EDITED BY
DR. HOWARD SCHROEDER, Ph.D.
Professor in Reading and Language Arts
Dept. of Curriculum and Instruction
Mankato State University

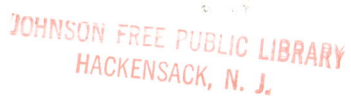
JOHNSON FREE PUBLIC LIBRARY
HACKENSACK, N. J.

CRESTWOOD HOUSE
Mankato, Minnesota

LIBRARY OF CONGRESS CATALOGING IN PUBLICATION DATA

Sanford, William R. (William Reynolds).
  The pelicans.

  (Wildlife, habits & habitat)
  Includes index.
  SUMMARY: Discusses the physical characteristics, habitat, behavior, and life cycle of one of the world's largest waterbirds.
  1. Brown pelican--Juvenile literature. (1. Brown pelican. 2. Pelicans.) I. Green, Carl R. II. Schroeder, Howard. III. Title. IV. Series.
  QL696.P47S26   1987   598.4'3   87-22251
  ISBN 0-89686-337-9

International Standard Book Number:	Library of Congress Catalog Card Number:
Library Binding 0-89686-337-9	87-22251

CREDITS

Illustrations:
Cover Photo: Don and Pat Valenti/Tom Stack & Associates
Leonard Lee Rue III: 4
Jim Brandenburg/DRK Photo: 7, 27
Dominique Braud/Tom Stack & Associates: 9
John Shaw/Tom Stack & Associates: 10
Tom Bledsoe/DRK Photo: 13
Jack B. Huhnerkoch: 15
Lynn M. Stone: 17, 18, 22, 24-25, 29, 37, 43, 44
Annie Griffiths/DRK Photo: 33
M. Philip Kahl, Jr./DRK Photo: 35
David Phillips: 41
Andy Schlabach: 45
Graphic Design & Production:
Baker Street Productions, Ltd.

Copyright© 1987 by Crestwood House, Inc. All rights reserved. No part of this book may be reproduced in any form without written permission from the publisher, except for brief passages included in a review. Printed in the United States of America.

Hwy. 66 South, Box 3427
Mankato, MN 56002-3427

TABLE OF CONTENTS

Introduction 5
    A wonderful bird is the pelican

Chapter One: A close-up look at the brown pelican 8
    A colorful bird
    The pelican's all-purpose bill
    A fleshy fishnet
    Built for sea and air

Chapter Two: The brown pelican's coastal habitat 16
    A diet of fish and more fish
    Strong, graceful flyers
    Catching fish in a pouch
    Only the nesting chicks are noisy
    A pelican faces many dangers

Chapter Three: The life cycle of the brown pelican 26
    Three new chicks
    Feeding chicks is a full-time job
    Growing flight feathers
    Flapper's first flight
    Flying south
    Courting and nest-building

Chapter Four: The pelican has been around for a long time 34
    Ancient myths don't always agree
    Pelicans can figure things out
    The nation's first wildlife refuge
    A new threat to the pelican

Chapter Five: The pelican's battle with DDT 39
    A troubling discovery
    The villain was DDT
    DDT enters the food chain
    Danger of extinction
    Will we win the next battle?

Map: 45
Index/Glossary: 46-47

In its own special way, the pelican is a beautiful creature.

INTRODUCTION:

"Homework is for the birds," Brian muttered. He crumpled a math paper into a ball and threw it at the trash basket.

Tracy looked up from her work and smiled at her twin. "You're lucky you don't have to do my homework," she said. "Ms. Vincent told us to choose our favorite poems. Do you think she'll like this limerick?"

Brian stared at her. "A limerick isn't serious poetry, Tracy. Ms. Vincent won't like it if it makes the class laugh."

Tracy didn't look worried. "Don't worry, this is a famous limerick. It was written by Dixon Lanier Merritt in 1910. It's about the pelican." She recited the poem from memory.

A wonderful bird is the pelican.
His bill will hold more than his belican.
　He can take in his beak
　Food enough for a week,
But I'm darned if I see how the helican.

"I guess Ms. Vincent might let you get away with that," Brian said. "It's almost as funny as the pelicans I saw last summer when I went fishing at the pier. They almost tripped over their bills as they waddled along!"

Tracy shook her head. "I think pelicans are beautiful in their own special way. They may look funny, but the design can't be too bad. Fossils tell us that pelicans haven't changed much throughout the years. I know, because I wrote about them last year for my science project.''

"I prefer birds that look like birds!" Brian said. "With those long bills and silly throat pouches, pelicans look like they belong in the age of dinosaurs."

"Think of it this way," Tracy replied. "About two million different species of birds have lived on earth since the first bird learned to fly. Less than one percent of those species are alive today—and the pelican is one of them. That's not bad for a 'living dinosaur,' is it?"

"Okay, I admit that the pelican's a tough old bird. But I can't believe that people really like them," Brian added.

Tracy dug out her old report. She flipped it open and read, "'The pelican is Louisiana's state bird, and the state's nickname is the Pelican State. Sailors name their ships after pelicans, and there are dozens of islands named for them.'" She looked up. "Have you heard of Alcatraz Island in San Francisco Bay?"

"Sure, who hasn't?" Brian said. "There used to be a federal prison there."

"It's really Pelican Island!" Tracy shot back. "Alcatraz is Spanish for pelican." She turned a page. "'In Pakistan, pelicans are a symbol of peace. That makes sense, because pelicans seldom fight with other birds. They seem content to live and let live.'"

Brian put up his hands and said, "I give up. Let me read your report. If the pelican's such a great bird, I might as well learn some more about it."

Pelicans glide smoothly through the air.

CHAPTER ONE:

The name "pelican" probably comes from the Greek word *pelekys,* which means ax. The Greeks used pelekys to refer to woodpeckers. It was the English who looked at the pelican's bill and called it by the Greek word. Despite the name, a pelican's bill is useless for drilling holes or chopping wood.

Pelicans are part of an order of water birds known as the *Pelecaniformes.* Other members of the order include the booby, the cormorant, and the frigatebird. Most *Pelecaniformes* like a warm climate, but some species summer in cooler regions.

The pelican's own family is called the Pelecanidae. Of the family's seven species, only the brown pelican and the American white pelican live in the Americas. The four European pelicans are the Eastern white, the Dalmatian, the pink-backed, and the grey. Australia and New Guinea have their own species, known as the Australian pelican. All pelicans have long bills and throat pouches, but they vary greatly in size and color.

The American white pelican *(Pelecanus erythrorhynchos)* may well be the world's largest water bird. This pelican has a wingspan of ten feet (3 m) from wingtip to wingtip and weighs up to twenty pounds (9 kg). As its name suggests, this freshwater pelican has a handsome coat of white feathers. When it spreads its wings, black flight feathers show up. These feathers make the

The American white pelican is one of the world's largest water birds.

wings look as if they've been dipped in black paint.

The wingspan of the smaller brown pelican *(P. occidentalis)* averages eight to nine feet (2.4 to 2.7 m). A typical bird measures fifty inches (1.3 m) from the tip of its twelve-inch (30 cm) bill to its webbed feet. A bird that size weighs eight to ten pounds (3.6 to 4.5 kg). Most females are only about three-fourths the size of the males, but they have the same plumage.

Although the brown pelican is smaller than the white one, its wingspan is up to nine feet (2.7 m) wide.

Unlike the white pelican, the brown pelican is a saltwater bird. It's also different in that it catches fish by skydiving from as high as forty feet (12 m). The family is made up of four subspecies, each of which occupies a different habitat. The best-known brown pelicans are the eastern brown *(P. o. carolinensis)* and the California brown *(P. o. californicus)*. The California brown pelican is the larger of the two.

A colorful bird

A California brown pelican has large, coarse feathers that change colors with the seasons. In summer, the brown pelican wears silver-grey feathers on its back and wings. Its neck is a rich dark brown and its head is white. The feathers that cover its chest and stomach are a dark, purplish grey. In the early fall, the pelican replaces its old feathers in a process called molting. After molting, its new feathers feature a showy band of white on the neck, and a crown of gold on the head. These color changes signal that the pelican is ready to mate.

Seasonal colors also show up elsewhere on the pelican. The bill changes from chalky white to red-gold. The pouch turns a dark grey with reddish undertones (olive green on the eastern brown pelican). Finally, the tissue around the bird's light blue eyes takes on a reddish-pink color.

Only the parent birds could love a newly hatched pelican chick. Veins throb under naked dark-grey skin. As the days go by, the chicks put on a coat of soft white down. At three weeks, they sprout their first feathers. Until their feathers grow in fully at eleven weeks, the chicks cannot fly. Half-grown birds (known as juveniles) have white feathers on their chest and grey-brown feathers on their necks, head, back, and wings.

The pelican's all-purpose bill

Without its bill, a pelican would be helpless. This all-purpose tool is the pelican's hand, fishnet handle, and comb. As a hand, the bill picks up food and builds nests. As a fishnet handle, the bill opens wide to scoop fish into the pouch. Finally, as a comb, the bill takes oil from a gland near the bird's tail to clean and waterproof each feather. This process, called preening, also kills bacteria and fungi.

A brown pelican's bill can be as long as eighteen inches (46 cm). Slender and strong, it ends in a clawlike hook. The two rami (branches) that make up the lower half of the bill join only at the tip. This arrangement allows the pelican to spread the rami and provides an opening to the pelican's famous pouch.

A fleshy fishnet

The pouch is a flexible, three-layered bag of skin. It folds neatly under the bill when the pelican is flying. When a pelican dives, it scoops fish and water into the pouch. An adult bird can hold up to two gallons of water (7.6 liters) in its pouch. After the pelican surfaces, it closes its bill. Strong muscles force the water out through the corners of its mouth. Only the fish are left

A pelican's bill is a handy tool for fishing, building nests, and preening.

inside this fleshy fishnet.

Pelicans must swallow their catch before they fly again. If they didn't, the weight of fish in the pouch would unbalance the bird and make flight impossible. When feeding its chicks, the parent bird regurgitates half-digested food into its pouch. The pouch then becomes a dinner bowl. The hungry chicks nearly bury themselves in the pouch in their eagerness to feed.

Built for sea and air

Pelicans look clumsy on land because nature gave them short legs and webbed feet. Because of this, they waddle like a duck when they walk. Ducks and other water birds have three toes, but pelicans have four toes and three areas of thick webbing. The third toe also has a long claw. The pelican uses the claw for scratching and for preening feathers that it can't reach with its bill. Despite the webbing, the feet are flexible. A pelican can perch easily on a tree limb or on the edge of its nest.

In the air, the brown pelican loses its clumsy look. Its big body is supported by hollow bones that are strong without being heavy. Powerful flight muscles move its long, tapered wings in sweeping strokes. The feet fold up and the bill settles back against the crooked neck.

Keen eyes scan the ocean for the silvery gleam of fish. When the pelican dives, it hits the water hard.

The pelicans' short legs make them look very clumsy on land.

Because its nostrils (located at the tip of the bill) are blocked to keep out water, it breathes through the corners of its mouth. Heavy bones in the head and a layer of air sacs under the skin cushion the shock from the dive. The air sacs also keep the pelican afloat.

If you want to see these wonderful birds in action, head for the ocean. The brown pelican can be found wherever there are warm waters and fish to catch.

CHAPTER TWO:

The brown pelican ranges up and down the coasts of North and South America. On the Pacific coast, the California brown pelican can be found as far north as British Columbia and as far south as Chile. On the Atlantic coast, the eastern brown pelican is seldom seen farther north than North Carolina. Its southern limit is Guyana on the northern coast of South America. Brown pelicans are nearly extinct along the Louisiana and Texas coasts.

Many brown pelicans migrate in the summer to find better fishing waters. These flights seldom cover more than a few hundred miles. If the birds do migrate, they return to home waters in the fall, where they mate and raise their chicks. A favorite breeding ground for eastern brown pelicans is Pelican Island off the Florida coast. California browns favor breeding grounds on islands off the coasts of southern California and Baja California (a peninsula between the Pacific Ocean and the Gulf of California).

A diet of fish and more fish

Brown pelicans depend on fish—a lot of fish—to live. A chick needs four pounds (1.8 kg) of food a day. That adds up to 150 pounds (68 kg) of fish by the time a juvenile learns to feed itself. For their part, adult birds eat up to twenty percent of their weight each day.

Pelicans usually feed on schools of small fish. In order to find a school, pelicans will fly as far as twenty-five miles (40 km) and back. Fish have mysterious habits, however. It's not unusual for the schools to suddenly disappear. When that happens, thousands of pelicans and other seabirds face starvation.

Commercial fishers once complained that pelicans ate too many of the fish that humans eat. They used

Pelicans dive fast and hard into the water, catching the fish by surprise.

17

Cruising at twenty-five (40 km) miles per hour, pelicans make flying look easy.

that argument as an excuse for killing pelicans. But naturalists proved that the fishers were wrong. Studies showed that pelicans eat fish that humans don't eat. These "trash fish" include menhaden, mullet, toadfish, pinfish, and topminnow. When pelicans do go after food fish, they seem to favor anchovies and sardines.

Strong, graceful flyers

Brown pelicans are strong and graceful flyers, but taking off is hard work. Because of their weight, they need the extra lift they receive by facing into the wind. If they're flying off the ocean, pelicans flap their wings hard and paddle madly with their webbed feet. When flying from the ground, they need a short run into the wind to get airborne.

Once in the air, pelicans make flying look easy. On a long flight, the birds fly at a cruising speed of twenty-five miles (40 km) per hour. Sometimes a flock flies in a V formation, but more often the birds fly in a long, angled line. Each bird's passage disturbs the air and lowers wind resistance. Thus, the pelicans behind benefit from the work done by those ahead. Because the lead position is the most tiring, the birds take turns flying in front. If head winds are a problem, the flock may dip down to sea level. At zero altitude, they fly in the wind-free troughs between the waves.

Wise old sailors say that pelicans can foretell the weather. If pelicans aren't flying, or if they desert their resting spot in a harbor, there's usually a storm coming. Pelicans also are experts at finding the rising columns of warm air called thermals. Pilots have seen pelicans ride a good thermal to altitudes of several thousand feet.

Catching fish in a pouch

White pelicans favor a fishing method seldom used by brown pelicans. The whites gather on the surface of a lake in a large circle. Then, with a great flapping of wings, they herd the fish they've trapped into a smaller and smaller space. When the circle is tight enough, the pelicans scoop up their dinner. Brown pelicans prefer to dive on the fish from the air.

Diving requires both timing and skill. From the air, the pelican must figure out the size, speed, and depth of the target fish. As it plummets down at sixty miles (97 km) per hour, the pelican adjusts its dive by moving its half-folded wings. Its feet act like the braking flaps on an airplane. If the fish swim out of range, the pelican levels out and flies off to try again.

At the moment it hits the water, the pelican thrusts its wings and legs back against its body. The force of the impact stuns the fish who are swimming there. The pelican opens its bill and gathers its catch into its pouch. While it's underwater, the pelican somersaults so that it surfaces with its head into the wind. If something frightens the pelican soon after it has eaten, it quickly regurgitates the meal. Naturalists think that this lightens the bird's load and permits a faster takeoff.

Most of the fish the pelican goes after swim close to the surface. That requires a dive that starts from a height of ten to twenty feet (3 to 6 m). To dive deeper, the pelican starts at a higher altitude. The pelican is careful not to take a fish larger than its bill. Bigger fish can choke a careless pelican. For a similar reason, the pelican swallows fish headfirst. If a fish went down tail first, the fins would catch in the bird's throat.

Only the nesting chicks are noisy

Only when they're chicks do pelicans make much noise. The nestlings peep and squawk all day long. A colony of adult birds may go weeks without making a single sound. They break this rule of silence only when they're nesting. The sitting bird makes a single deep cluck when its mate arrives to take over the nest.

Brown pelicans prefer nesting sites near the sea, where predators are few. In Florida, they nest in mangrove trees. If a tree isn't available, the birds nest on the ground. They build round nests, about two feet (61 cm) across and five inches (13 cm) high. Each nest is made of sticks, reeds, leaves, and branches, and it's lined with grass. Two weeks after the nest is built, the female lays two or three three-inch (7.6 cm) chalky white eggs. They hatch about a month later.

A hungry chick reaches into its mother's pouch for a fish dinner.

A pelican faces many dangers

From the moment it hatches, a pelican chick's life is in danger. If the parents don't bring enough food, it will die. Some chicks fall out of the nest and can't get back. Others are eaten by sea lions, fish crows, gulls, or other predators. A storm may send waves crashing over the nest, or a swarm of mosquitos may drive the parents away. But once a pelican is grown, its only natural enemies are sharks and internal parasites.

The big seabirds aren't so lucky when it comes to humans. Very few people would kill a pelican on purpose. But pelicans often get caught on fishhooks or tangled up on fishing lines. The plastic rings that hold six-packs of cold drinks are dangerous, too. Many pelicans have starved to death after getting the rings caught on their bills.

Environmental dangers also threaten the pelican. In Florida, for example, nesting areas in the Everglades are drying up. Canals are taking water to dry farmlands, or carrying it out to the ocean. Another danger lies in oil spills. When a seabird's feathers are coated with oil, it loses its ability to fly.

Despite these dangers, pelicans may live twenty years or more. One captive pelican lived for thirty years in a zoo. During their long life, the birds follow a life cycle that is well adapted to their marine habitat.

Pelicans live in harmony with their marine habitat.

CHAPTER THREE:

The young naturalist swats a mosquito and squints through her binoculars. The sun is climbing into a cloudless Florida sky, but Suzanne hardly notices. She's speaking softly into her tape recorder. After weeks of waiting, Nosey and Bomber's eggs are about to hatch.

Suzanne feels as though her blind on this little island is a second home. She's been coming here for a year now to study a colony of eastern brown pelicans. Across the Indian River, she can see the beaches of the barrier and the mainland. Suddenly, she sits up straighter. Bomber is swooping down to a perfect landing beside his nest.

Three new chicks

Bomber takes Nosey's place and settles himself on three precious eggs. After her years of study, Suzanne knows what's happening. Nosey laid the three white eggs in March. That was a month ago. Inside each egg, a pelican chick now is chipping away at the shell with its egg tooth. The egg tooth is a hard calcium point on the tip of the baby bird's bill. The tooth drops off a few days after the chick hatches.

The first chick breaks free of the shell in just over

two hours. The other two chicks take ten and twelve hours, which is more common. The first chick is a three-ounce (85 g) male. The tiny, naked hatchling tries to stand, but he can barely lift his head. Even so, his squawks carry across the mangrove swamp. Pelican chicks are quiet only when they're asleep. Suzanne decides to call him Flapper.

The next two chicks are both females. Suzanne names them Downy and Fluff. The parent birds take turns shading the chicks from the bright sun. Left unshaded for more than a few minutes, the chicks would die. Nosey and Bomber also guard the nest against hungry crows and gulls.

After breaking through its shell, this tiny hatchling takes a rest.

Feeding chicks is a full-time job

Guard duty is only a small part of the job. The chicks are always hungry. For the first ten days, the parents feed them by dribbling half-digested fish into the nest. The chicks gobble the gooey mess and want more. At ten days, they're strong enough to reach into their parents' pouches for food. Bomber and Nosey never force food into the chicks' mouths. Pelican chicks that can't feed themselves will die.

Flapper always grabs more than his share. He's soon much bigger than Downy and Fluff. Fluff isn't strong enought to fight for her share. Suzanne knows what's coming, but there's nothing she can do. In the wild, life belongs to the strong. A day later, the larger chicks crowd Fluff out of the nest. She dies in the tangle of roots at the foot of the tree.

Growing flight feathers

Flapper and Downy grow rapidly on their fish diet. By the time they're three weeks old, Flapper weighs three pounds (1.4 kg). Downy is smaller, but she fights like a tiger for her share of the food. Both chicks now have a fluffy coat of wooly white down. At three and a half weeks, they sprout dark feathers on their wingtips and shoulders.

As the flight feathers develop, the chicks also grow their light-brown back plumage. When they're not demanding food, they sit beside the nest and flap their wings. They don't pay much attention to the colony of pelican chicks whose nests are on the ground. These chicks gather in a squawking mob when their parents are gone. They rush toward any adult that lands, but the older birds know their own chicks. They refuse to feed anyone else.

The chicks grow fast.

Flapper's first flight

At eleven weeks, Flapper and Downy are fully feathered juveniles. Bomber and Nosey coax them to take their first flight. The young ones flap and flex their wings, but they hold fast to the tree. Finally, Flapper faces into a stiff breeze and launches himself into the air. The first flight is short and clumsy. It ends with a crash landing in the water.

Slowly, both pelicans learn the skills they'll need as adults. They take off and land without crashing. Once in the air, they master the easy, gliding flight of the pelican. Most of all, they begin to learn the art of fishing. This is a life-or-death matter, for Bomber and Nosey will soon stop feeding their juvenile chicks. When they do, the young birds must live on stored-up fat until they can catch their own fish.

At first, Flapper and Downy come up empty every time they plunge into the water. Finally, Flapper plunges into the middle of a school of minnows. He surfaces with a pouch full of wiggling little fish. Downy is right behind him, and she feeds well, too. Within the week, both birds join older pelicans as they fly out over the ocean on longer fishing trips.

Flying south

When fall arrives, Flapper joins a flock of older birds on a flight south to the Florida Keys. Here, the warm waters of the Gulf Stream provide good fishing. The young pelican is now catching fish seven dives out of ten. Flapper puts on weight, especially after he finds a new food source.

Each morning, Flapper flies to a fishing pier. He picks up an easy meal when people throw scraps of fish into the water. Small gulls circle around, but he ignores them. One brave gull lands on his head and steals a fish from his bill. The even-tempered Flapper doesn't seem to be upset by the daring thief. He flies up to the pier and takes a sunbath on a piling.

Flapper stays in the Keys for three years. He's now fully mature. When spring comes again, instinct tells him that it's time to fly north. A slow and easy flight takes him back to the small island on which he was hatched. A colony of pelicans is nesting there, but Flapper finds a mangrove tree to call his own.

Courting and nest-building

Watching from her blind, Suzanne sees Flapper begin his courtship dance. Flapper swings his head back and forth like a giant pendulum. A young female named Kelly soon shows some interest. When the female waddles toward him, Flapper snaps at her. Kelly turns her head to one side to show that she isn't a threat.

When Kelly comes closer, Flapper doesn't snap. Instead, he flies to another tree and returns with a dead branch. Kelly accepts the branch as a kind of wedding gift. Then she flies down to the water. Flapper follows her. They touch bills and wings with great gentleness. Finally they mate.

For the next week, Flapper brings nesting materials and Kelly arranges them. If Flapper puts a twig in the wrong place, Kelly moves it. A fight breaks out when another pelican tries to steal branches from Flapper's nest. With a clash of bills, Flapper drives the thief away. When the nest is complete, Kelly settles down to lay her eggs.

With luck, the pair will stay together for many years. They may move their nesting place, but it won't be far from the island. As Suzanne watches the young pair, she tells herself, "Let's hope that builders don't decide to put up apartments here. Pelicans can survive anything except too many people."

A pair of pelicans raise their young.

CHAPTER FOUR:

Is the pelican a clown or a superstar? Most people have trouble making up their minds. With its dinosaur bill and crooked neck, the pelican does look funny as it waddles across a pier. But watch a flight of pelicans soar gracefully overhead. Their great wings beat in almost perfect time with the leader. In the air, the pelican is clearly a superstar.

Ancient myths don't always agree

The ancients also saw the pelican in different ways. In Egypt, the pelican was a symbol for foolish behavior. That was because the females sometimes laid their eggs on the ground. In a similar way, Europeans of the Middle Ages called people "pelicans" if they ate and talked too much. In truth, pelicans are greedy eaters. But only the chicks can be accused of "talking" too much.

By contrast, the early Christian church saw the pelican as a symbol of Christ's sacrifice. That belief was based on an old folktale. The story said that female pelicans fed their chicks with their own blood if they couldn't catch enough fish. Even though the story was false, pelicans appear often in church art. The long-

Sailors often named their ships after pelicans, hoping it would bring them good luck.

billed birds show up in stained glass, on carved panels, and perched on top of wooden crosses.

For their part, sailors envied the way pelicans ride so lightly on the waves. They often named their ships after them, hoping that the name would give them luck. Perhaps the belief had some value. The second ship to sail around the world started its life as the *Pelican*. But Sir Francis Drake renamed it before he sailed. The ship went down in history as the *Golden Hind*.

Pelicans can figure things out

Where pelicans are protected, they soon lose much of their fear of people. In Sarasota, Florida, Dale Shields runs a hospital for injured pelicans. When his birds recover, they often hang around like old friends. Even after they fly away, some come back each year for a visit—and a free meal.

In 1987, some brown pelicans showed even more intelligence. The incident started with an oil spill near Jacksonville, Florida. Naturalists set up a rescue station to wash the oil off the seabirds that were caught in the spill. They caught and cleaned many birds, but no pelicans. Then, all at once, fifty-two pelicans waddled into the station. It was as if they had been waiting their turn for a cleanup.

The nation's first wildlife refuge

Pelican Island lies near Florida's famous Cape Kennedy rocket base. It is a small island that measures only three and a half acres (1.4 hectares) at low tide. Despite its small size, Pelican Island is famous. It was the first wildlife refuge set up by the federal government. The government now owns more than three hundred wildlife refuges.

In the early 1900's, pelicans were being killed for their large flight feathers. Designers wanted the feathers for making women's hats. Members of the National Audubon Society and the American Ornithologist's Union worried that the pelican was becoming an endangered species. They took the problem to President Theodore Roosevelt. Because of his great interest in wildlife, the President understood the problem. In 1903, he set Pelican Island aside as a bird sanctuary under

These pelicans gather for a free lunch.

the Department of Agriculture.

Since then, the brown pelicans that nest on Pelican Island are very safe. No one is allowed to change or destroy anything on the island. In addition, as part of the National Wilderness System, the island is closed to visitors. Similar laws protect all pelicans in Florida. No one may hunt, capture, sell, or keep a pelican as a pet.

Ornithologists (naturalists who study birds) keep a close watch on Pelican Island. If they see a bird that is injured or sick, they pick it up and treat it. Once the bird is well, the ornithologists fasten an aluminum band around the pelican's leg. Anyone who sees a banded pelican is asked to contact the Fish and Wildlife Service in Washington, D.C. Scientists at the Bird Banding lab in Maryland use the data to trace the life story of each banded pelican.

A new threat to the pelican

Despite these efforts, pelicans came face-to-face with a deadly new danger in the 1960's. Naturalists noticed that pelicans were disappearing from their usual habitats. The losses sounded an alarm that woke up bird lovers everywhere. But no one knew what was happening. Naturalists feared that the pelican might become extinct before they learned the name of the enemy.

CHAPTER FIVE:

Anacapa Island lies just nine miles (14.5 km) off the coast of California. For many years, Anacapa and the other Channel Islands have been a favorite breeding ground for the California brown pelican. The island's cliffs provide good nesting sites and the nearby kelp beds attract large schools of fish.

A troubling discovery

In March of 1969, naturalists from the University of California visited Anacapa. They found three hundred pairs of pelicans nesting on one part of the island. A closer look, however, turned up a problem. Most of the nests were empty. If a nest had eggs in it, the eggs had been crushed. Only a few nests held unbroken eggs.

The naturalists saw that the damage hadn't been done by predators. Instead, the eggs broke when the pelicans tried to incubate them. Tests showed that the eggshells were only half as thick as usual. A second visit several weeks later showed that all the eggs were broken. No pelican chicks were hatched on Anacapa Island in 1969.

The villain was DDT

Chemical tests soon pointed to the cause. A pesticide called DDT was at fault. Pelicans and other birds that ate fish with a high DDT content were affected. The chemical kept the females from laying eggshells that could support their weight.

At first, no one wanted to believe the news. DDT was one of the miracles of the modern age. Farmers were spraying DDT on their fields to kill crop-destroying insects. More importantly, millions of lives were saved when DDT wiped out disease-carrying insects. Malaria, dysentery, and typhus were all being brought under control.

DDT enters the food chain

The problem with DDT was that it didn't disappear after it did its job. Once farmers sprayed DDT on their fields, the chemical entered the food chain. Animals that ate plants sprayed with DDT stored the chemical in the fatty tissues of their bodies. If predators ate these birds and mammals, the chemical built up in their bodies, too.

DDT didn't stop with the damage it did on land. Water ran off from the fields and carried DDT into lakes, rivers, and oceans. In the ocean, the chemical was absorbed by tiny animals called plankton. Scientists found that plankton built up DDT levels a hundred times greater than that of the seawater. The tiny marine animals that ate the plankton and the fish that ate the tiny animals stored an even greater amount of DDT. At the end of the food chain were the brown pelicans. When the birds ate the fish, they absorbed a large dose of the pesticide.

DDT didn't kill the pelicans. Instead, it kept them from holding calcium carbonate in their bodies. Lack-

The normal eggs of a pelican are shown above. In the late 1960's, DDT caused female pelicans to lay eggs with thin shells.

ing calcium, the females laid eggs with paper-thin shells. When they tried to incubate the eggs, they crushed them. Pelicans can cope with a DDT level of 2.5 parts per million. The Anacapa birds, however, were carrying twenty-seven times more DDT than was safe.

Danger of extinction

The message was clear: The California brown pelican had become an endangered species. Other naturalists reported that brown pelicans were almost extinct in Texas and Louisiana. Farmers there were using large amounts of DDT and another pesticide named Endrin on their crops. The pattern was the same in Florida and off the coast of Baja California.

In 1972, the United States took action. The government outlawed the use of DDT. Many countries followed the lead of the United States, but not all. Some nations in Asia, Africa, and Latin America still use the pesticide. In the countries that stopped, however, the DDT in the soil began to decrease.

Will we win the next battle?

Luckily, the brown pelican didn't give up. On North Coronado Island, near San Diego, California, not a single pelican hatched in 1969. But the adults kept trying. By 1974, naturalists counted more than a thousand young pelicans in the nests there. The California brown pelican was on its way back. Along the Gulf coast, however, the eastern brown pelican has been slower to recover.

Naturalists remind us that DDT isn't the only threat to our marine wildlife. Oil spills can also do terrible damage. Sewage and other wastes dumped into the sea can pollute the water, and cause birds, fish, and plants to die.

Good detective work and new laws saved the brown pelican, but what does the future hold? The experience of the pelican shows us that taking care of the environment is an important job—and one in which everyone has a part.

In 1972, the United States took action to save the brown pelican.

A pelican enjoys a quiet moment at sunset.

MAP:

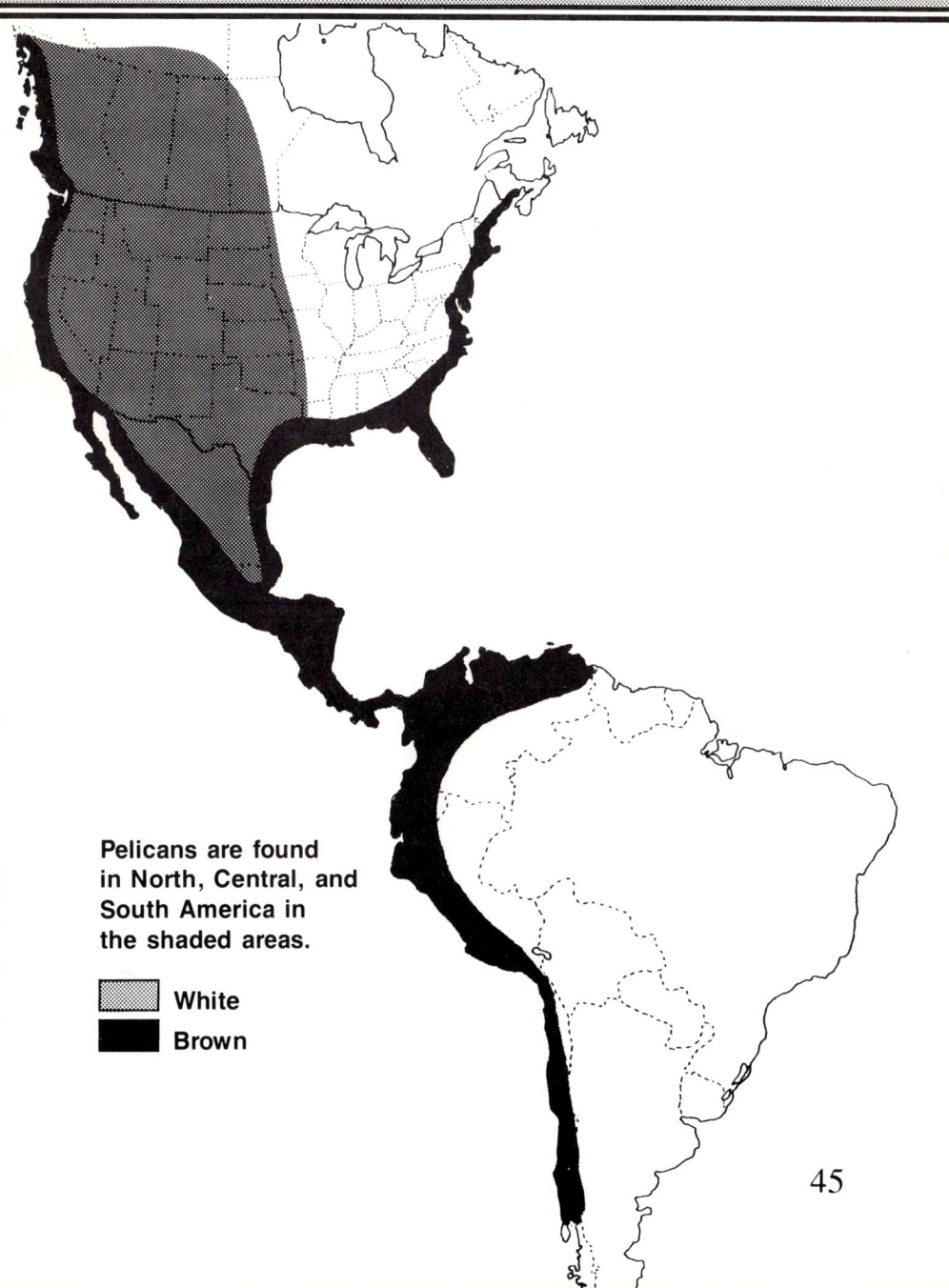

Pelicans are found in North, Central, and South America in the shaded areas.

▧ White
■ Brown

INDEX/GLOSSARY:

AIR SACS 15 — *Pockets of air found under the skin of a pelican. Air sacs cushion the shock when a pelican hits the water.*

BEHAVIOR 12, 20, 21, 26, 27

BLIND 26, 31 — *A hiding place from which one may observe wildlife.*

CHICK 11, 14, 16, 21, 23, 26, 27, 28, 29, 30, 34, 39 — *A newly hatched male or female pelican.*

COLOR 8, 11, 28

DIET 16, 17, 28

DDT 40, 41, 42, 43 — *A powerful pesticide. DDT enters the food chain and causes birds to lay thin-shelled eggs that can't be incubated.*

DOWN 11, 29 — *The soft, fluffy feathers of a pelican chick.*

EGG TOOTH 26 — *A hard, pointed bit of calcium found on the tip of an unhatched pelican chick's bill. The chick uses the egg tooth to break its way out of the egg.*

ENDANGERED SPECIES 37, 42 — *An animal that is in danger of becoming extinct.*

ENEMIES 23, 40, 41, 42, 43

EXTINCTION 16, 38, 42 — *The loss of a species, as when the last animal of that species dies.*

FLIGHT FEATHERS 29, 37 — *The large, stiff feathers found in a bird's wings and tail. Birds can't fly without flight feathers.*

HABITAT 10, 23, 24, 38 — *The place where an animal makes its home.*

INCUBATION 39, 42 — *The process of keeping eggs warm so that they will hatch.*

JUVENILES 11, 17, 30 — *Half-grown pelican chicks.*

MATING 11, 16, 21, 26, 31, 32

MIGRATION 16 — *The yearly movement of animals from one habitat area to another.*

MOLTING 11 — *When a bird loses its feathers and new feathers grow to replace them.*

NATURALIST 18, 20, 26, 36, 38, 39, 42, 43 — *A scientist who studies animals and plants.*

INDEX/GLOSSARY:

ORNITHOLOGIST 37, 38 — *A naturalist who is an expert on birds.*

PESTICIDE 40, 41, 42 — *A poison used to kill insect pests.*

PHYSICAL CHARACTERISTICS 11, 12, 14, 15, 19, 27

PLUMAGE 9, 29 — *A bird's feathers.*

PREDATOR 21, 23, 39, 40 — *An animal that lives by preying on other animals.*

PREENING 12, 14 — *When a pelican uses its bill to clean, smooth, and waterproof its feathers.*

RAMI 12 — *The two branches that make up the lower half of a pelican's bill. The rami open to provide entry to the pouch.*

RANGE 16, 20

REGURGITATE 14, 20 — *To vomit partly digested food.*

SEABIRD 17, 23, 36 — *Any bird that lives in a marine habitat.*

SENSES 14

SIZE 8, 9, 12, 27

SOUNDS 21, 29

THROAT POUCH 6, 8, 11, 12, 14, 20, 28, 30 — *The large, fleshy bag that hangs below a pelican's bill. The pouch serves the pelican as a net for catching fish.*

TRASH FISH 18 — *Any species of fish that people don't use as food.*

WEIGHT 8, 9, 28

WILDLIFE REFUGE 36, 37 — *A protected area where wild animals can live naturally and safely.*

WINGSPAN 8, 9 — *The distance from the tip of one outstretched wing to the other.*

READ AND ENJOY THE SERIES:

If you would like to know more about all kinds of wildlife, you should take a look at the other books in this series.

You'll find books on bald eagles and other birds. Books on alligators and other reptiles. There are books about deer and other big-game animals. And there are books about sharks and other creatures that live in the ocean.

In all of the books you will learn that life in the wild is not easy. But you will also learn what people can do to help wildlife survive. So read on!

J598.2 Copy 1
Sanford
The Pelicans

Johnson Free Public Library

Hackensack, New Jersey   07601